THE FIVE DOLLAR JOURNEY

CHARTING A COURSE TO FINANCIAL SUCCESS BY INVESTING
FIVE DOLLARS A DAY

Written by: Anomaly

Copyright © 2017 by **Anomaly**

All rights reserved. No part of this publication may be reproduced, distributed or transmitted in any form or by any means, without prior written permission.

For information contact:
ANOMALY1977@OUTLOOK.COM

Design by mycustombookcover.com

ISBN: 978-1979648851

"As human beings, we have intelligence and courage. Provided we use these qualities, we will be able to achieve whatever we set out to do."

—DALAI LAMA

CONTENTS

PREFACE VII

INTRODUCTION: 1

SUCCESS: WHAT WE'VE ALL EXPERIENCED 5

THE GOAL 9

THE STRATEGY 13

TIME FOR SOME INCREASE 19

AIRBNB 21

RIDE SHARING 27

DELIVERY DRIVER 31

LANDSCAPING AND PROPERTY MAINTENANCE 35

TAKING PICTURES FOR BPO COMPANIES AND REAL ESTATE REFERRALS 39

TEACH SOMETHING YOU LOVE 45

YOUR $5 GOAL 47

THE $500/WEEK INVESTOR 53

IF AT FIRST YOU DON'T SUCCEED 57

THE VALUE OF EDUCATION 61

PREFACE

I've had the opportunity to learn so many things from my father who happened to be a great teacher and very positive role model for me. He had such great attributes and an obvious heart for humanity. One thing I really admired about my father was his willingness to help others in need. Throughout my life, I have come across many individuals who were good hearted but really struggled financially. Many of them were born into their situations. They had never been taught how to positively increase their wealth or even the basics on money management. Due to this lack of knowledge, they often became victims of an environment that reinforced financial decline.

Like my father, I got to a point where I wanted to help people: specifically, in experiencing financial success. I learned a few things from my father as far as the concepts of investing and having your money work for you. My readings of Robert Kiyosaki and Warren Buffet increased my knowledge and my drive for more financial literacy. I also listened to online discussions by Dr. Boyce Watkins as well as Dave Ramsey. Once I got to a certain place in my learning and began putting in place some of these concepts from the financial gurus I started seeing financial success. After several years of learning and applying these principles I got to a point where I wanted to make sure people were informed of the things that I learned. I wanted people to know there is a way out for the working poor and otherwise financially disenfranchised. There is a journey they could go on for $5/day.

INTRODUCTION

When I was younger, I remember seeing in the local store a magazine rack that had all kinds of financial magazines on it. They'd be mixed in near the motorcycle and sports magazines. The front cover of the money magazine usually had a picture of some guru bragging about his yacht or luxury car collection. There were times my father would pick up these magazines and look at them. Of course, I was just a kid so I was more interested in going outside to play. One day I asked him if the magazines were interesting at all. He said that a lot of times those magazines had good advice and that following that advice could make us rich. Well, that never happened. Part of the reason was because the methods these financial gurus talked about needed a certain level of money to even utilize them. In money lingo, it's referred to as Economy of scale. Economy of scale basically says that certain investment tools and resources are only available to a person at a certain financial status or level. It's like the saying you have to crawl before you can walk. In order to walk there's the building up of muscles and coordination that has to first take place. It's almost the same concept with money and investments. For example, there are investments for people who have an extra $5/day; investments for people who have an extra $500/week; investments for people who have an extra $5 Million/month. These are just examples. Just in case you're wondering, this book is more for the $5/day kind of investor. The aim of this book is to show you some ways to go from $0/day to $500/week.

    I remember this one time when my father was sitting in a chair, deep in thought. I said to him "Dad, are you OK?" He seemed a little startled when he heard my voice. I guess he didn't realize that he was so deep into thought. He said "Yeah...yeah, I'm ok. I was just thinking about something. I'm trying to think of a way to come up with $5000. If I can then we can put it in this investment which will grow to $1 million in 10 years." I mean it sounded promising to a young kid who didn't know any better. However, the reality of the situation was that we didn't have $5000 and my father was never able to come up with a way to get that amount, for that investment.

Fast forward to today, I've come across a lot of people who are looking for that same "$5000" to get started. The problem is that sitting around waiting for $5000 to fall from the sky won't give you the results you're probably looking for. For this reason, many people have just given up on the idea of having a successful life as well as achieving financial gain. There are a couple of key issues that keep people from reaching this goal. The first issue is what their idea of success is which is generally tied to how much material wealth can be accumulated. The second issue is that when it comes to improving our finances we think it's only for those individuals who are already rich. You know, the whole "rich get richer" thing. You may not know what economy of scales is but you indirectly agree with its concept when you make up in your mind that since you have always been broke you will therefore continue to be broke. It may be true that the rich getting richer but that doesn't mean that your financial situation is hopeless. Both of these issues regarding success and wealth building couldn't be further from the truth. Let me just say that most of us have already experienced success and generating wealth can be done by most people in America.

In this quick read I'm going to get rid of some extremely common myths about both success and wealth generation while at the same time offer very practical and doable solutions to build your finances. I will share with you a number of specific things I have incorporated in my life as well as other peoples' lives that has resulted in consistent financial increase. I strongly dislike when I'm reading something that points out a problem but doesn't offer any concrete solutions to resolve it. This will not be the case here. You *will* have a roadmap to get to the destination of financial progression. What is financial progression? Let me define it according to my own idea:

1. Getting to a place where your money is compounding with interest, dividends, and other investments. In other words, I want you to get to a place where your money is working for you. While you sleep or go to the beach or go to the good ol' 9-5 your money is growing.

2. Reaching a point where your job is not your only source of income and if you lost your job you could, at minimum, still maintain your essential needs.

3. Arriving to a financial destination where you go from making zero or small money investments and get you to a place which will bring you thousands of dollars in returns every month on your investments.

4. Ultimately financial progression is a mindset change. Even if you aren't making a lot of money currently, changing your pattern of thinking when it comes to money and financial success is *still* progress. Infact, it's really not the steps that I will lay out in this book which will bring about the greatest change. It is how you think about the steps and what you tell yourself about both your financial goals as well as your overall life goals.

The first several chapters are things you can do to increase the amount of money you're bringing in every day, week, or month. The second part of the book will provide guidance on what can be done with that increase in money. The main point is to get you into a position where your money is working for you. Money can be one of the hardest workers you'll ever come across because money doesn't sleep, take breaks, need benefits, etc. As a matter of fact when you get your money working for you it operates 24 hours/day and 7 days/week. So even while you're sleeping your money can be working.

CHAPTER ONE

SUCCESS: WHAT WE'VE ALL EXPERIENCED

"SUCCESS IS THE PROGRESSIVE REALIZATION OF A WORTHY GOAL OR IDEA." —EARL NIGHTINGALE

Many times, we stand in our own way of progress. We'll say to our self "I'd like to do this" or "I'd like to do that" but we'll never do it or even attempt to do it. It's like the 65-year-old person who's always spoken of getting their driver's license but has never signed up for the test. For many reasons doubt gets into our mind and stops real progress from happening. It's as if doubt or fear cripples us. Sometimes we feel like we have never seen success in our own lives and that success is somehow something completely alien and foreign to us. Maybe success is for everyone else except the person in the mirror. Either way, we end up never even trying to do whatever it is we had in our heart or mind.

All of us would like to achieve our dreams, desires, and goals. Whether it's making it onto the high school track team, finishing trade school or college, or becoming a professional athlete. Unfortunately, when doubt enters our hearts and minds achieving these desires becomes almost impossible. Doubt causes us to lose the race before it ever gets started. The general response to doubt is to have a negative attitude or unwillingness to even to carry out the steps needed to accomplish our goals. In the end, we end up sabotaging our own success.

If that wasn't enough, many of us measure our success in terms of financial gain or material possessions. We think the size of our bank account is the determining factor of how successful we are. Some of us also believe that fancy cars or name brand sneakers and clothing dictate the measure of our success: that it in some way validates who we are. This way of thinking could not be further from the truth. In fact, most people who adopt this pattern of thinking end up going broke trying to keep up with the Joneses or once they have acquired whatever their material desire is, still feel a sense of emptiness. Such views lead to a very pessimistic conclusion about our situation. We begin to think that our situation is hopeless because we have not yet obtained true success and therefore never will. Maybe we've seen sprinkles of success here and there but nothing long lasting; nothing that will take us to another progressive level.

Let's go to Earl Nightingale's definition of success. Success is the progressive realization of a worthy goal or idea. This means that virtually every single person has not only obtained success once but does so on a continuous basis. Let me explain with an example: let's say you want the latest designer outfit. You say to yourself, "I'm going to work this extra shift and save to make this happen." So, your goal has been set. You end up working the extra shifts and pulling the money together to get that designer outfit you wanted. You have now experienced success! Congratulations! That's a somewhat obvious example. Let's try another example that may not seem so obvious. Let's say you need to go grocery shopping. You've made your list, whether it be on your cell phone, in your mind, or on paper. Then you go to the store and pick up everything on that list. Congratulations, again! The goal was to get everything on that list and our hypothetical successful person did just that. The same thing can be said for the person who plans to wake up at 6 AM to go to work and does so. Maybe it's a Monday and maybe the person is a little groggy but *by* God he/she has done it!

They've started off their day with success. Their goal was to wake up at a certain time and that's exactly what happened. I can go on and on about all the various modes of success that we experience, not only throughout our life but on a daily basis, as well.

By using this definition of success, you can wake up every day knowing that whatever happens throughout the day you've managed to have success. Keep this definition in mind because we will be coming back to it in the subsequent chapters.

CHAPTER TWO

THE GOAL

"AS A MAN THINKETH IN HIS HEART, SO IS HE."
—KING SOLOMON IN THE BOOK OF PROVERBS

Let's say it's a beautiful sunny summer day. You and some buddies decide to go to the beach. The beach is about an hour away by car which is normally not an issue. Today unfortunately your car has a flat tire and the people at the tire shop have the same idea as you. The good folks at the tire shop decided to go to the beach which means the also but in doing so they left the tire shop will be closed. So now you have a place to go to but your car is out of commission. Your good friend who is pretty much like family tells you that you can use his car but he can't pick you up. However you have an emergency set of keys to his house and inside his house is where he keeps his extra car keys. Since your best friend can't pick you up, you'll have to figure out how to get to his house. The great thing is that he's about a five-minute bicycle ride away or a 15-minute walk away. You decide that since it's such a beautiful day and you could use the extra exercise to walk over to his house. Everything goes smooth and you get the spare keys to the car and you're on your way to pick up some of your other friends to hit the beach on that beautiful summer day. Wait a sec! How about the snacks and drinks? You have to call up one of your other friends, who you're on the way to pick up, to see if they can help out with some of the snacks. Of course, they agree and ask if on the way to the beach you can stop at the local grocery store to pick that stuff up. You then grab that friend as well as your other beach companions and before you get on the main road to the beach you stop at the store to pick up the food and drink.

Notice, when you woke up and saw what a beautiful day it was and decided to go to the beach, you didn't realize that there was all this extra stuff you had to do. One of the things that kept our hypothetical person motivated was keeping in mind the bigger picture, which was the goal of getting to the beach. All the other stuff that happened to him didn't mess with the main goal which was getting to the beach.

The main goal of this book is to get middle and working-class people to progress financially. The reader must understand that the only way this book will be affective is if they allow themselves to be put in a better financial position. But it is extremely important that you 1) set up your goal 2) Do your best not to look to the left or the right but forge ahead, especially when distractions come. Remember it doesn't take an abundance of wealth to get financially ahead. To be honest, there are a whole host of reasons and excuses not to pursue a goal of financial progression. Maybe you think that your job doesn't pay enough. Maybe you feel like you don't have enough time. You may even set a goal and decide to give it up because it takes away from your social or family life. Maybe you're a person of a particular faith who feels that taking on something additional, even for personal growth, will cause you to be too distracted from the practices that may go along with your belief system.

Before going any further, you have to ask yourself, "Do I want to be that person who continues to make excuses for their lack? Do I want to be that person who blames the culture, politics, capitalism, discrimination, and whatever else I can think of? Do I want to be that person who consistently makes goals but never follows through?" If your answer is "no" then continue reading. The strategies of financial progress and improvement that I will lay out in this book are going to be relatively easy but it will take some effort on your part. The challenge will not be coming up with ideas and goals, but rather not letting everyday life and the cares of the world distract you so much that you never even start the strategy needed to accomplish whatever goal you've thought of.

We'll take a dive into this strategy but I do want to nudge you a bit and urge you to not underestimate the importance of setting your goal. Think to yourself how much change for good can happen once you get to a better financial position. Set up your goal. Don't allow distractions to hold you back. Embrace that goal of financial progress and do your best not to look to the left or to the right but push ahead.

CHAPTER THREE

THE STRATEGY

"AS HUMAN BEINGS, WE HAVE INTELLIGENCE AND COURAGE. PROVIDED WE USE THESE QUALITIES, WE WILL BE ABLE TO ACHIEVE WHATEVER WE SET OUT TO DO."
—DALAI LAMA

The reason I felt the need to take so much time in defining success is because often, when we have to change our habits for the better we either don't muster up enough energy/motivation to make a big effort or we don't even bother to try, at all. The reason for this is directly related to our views of how successful we've been in life. We tell ourselves that we haven't had success and most likely won't have success, ever. This close minded and negative way of thinking keeps us in our situation without ever seeing any improvement and growth. Also, that logic explains why many of us continue to go around the same mountain over and over again. That mentality keeps us dating or marrying the wrong kind of people; keeps us having the same circle of friends that help hold us back. In the end, it actually keeps us from getting ahead financially and free from the rut we so desperately want to be out of.

We not only have to be bold enough to set our goal, in this case a financial one, but we also should have a full understanding that success has been and will continue to be a daily part of our lives. Once we realize this then we can better see how *financial* success can also become a daily/monthly/yearly part of our lives.

With that in mind let's dive into the strategy. Having a vision or goal is different from having a strategy. Your vision is where you want to go while your strategy is how you get there.

Remember back in chapter 2 the story of our hypothetical guy who wanted to get to the beach on a sunny day. A goal was clearly established but there were several strategies used to achieve this specific goal. Likewise, I'll highlight several strategies that I've used in my own life as well as what I've seen in others' lives that can be a possibility for you, as well. Keep in mind that each one of these strategies will be further explained in the following chapters. If you haven't already noticed, each chapter will consist of one or two specific strategies. This way you don't have to comb through the entire book if you want to go back later on to that strategy. Here they go:

1. Increase how much money you're bringing in while keeping the expenses the same and possibly even decreasing them.

2. Airbnb

3. Use of ride sharing such as Lyft or Uber.

4. Delivery driver

5. Landscaping and property maintenance

6. Taking pictures with your camera for foreclosure companies or BPO (Broker Price Opinion) companies.

7. Real estate referrals

8. Teach someone something you're passionate about.

9. Increase your learning

10. Invest your money in mutual fund apps (e.g. Acorns or Stash).

11. Invest your money with a mutual fund brokerage.

12. Invest your money in real estate.

These above listed strategies are based on my own personal experiences, or the experiences of others I have interviewed. These are not the only examples you can use. There are other ways to bring about financial progress and growth and plenty of other financial experts who have ways they feel are better for getting you where you would like to be. These are just the ways that I know of, personally. I cannot guarantee that if you follow you will get to the next level. I am, however, providing a roadmap that will help you navigate through your financial journey.

Going back to the Dalai Lama's words: "As human beings we have intelligence and courage. Provided we use these qualities, we will be able to achieve whatever we set out to do." I can lay out the strategy for you as far as getting you from a $0/week investor to a $500/week investor and you may think the ideas are worthwhile which requires a degree of intelligence. You must have the courage to actually start to apply these things to your own life. There's a place in the Bible that says, "Faith without works is dead." - The Apostle James

Basically, this book can lay out a way to start moving closer to your financial goals but it's up to you to act on those strategies. If you don't it'll be another dead goal. You'll need courage to push against the doubt and the close mindedness that may have become a part of your everyday life. You may have to wake up a little earlier or go to bed a little later but keep in mind the bigger picture, which is the goal. Be forewarned: there will be naysayers. It's common for these people to be made up of family and friends. Does it mean they don't love you or like you? No, not at all. However just how you might be coming out of your habits or way of thinking to better yourself and others around you, they may not be at that point. So what you are doing may seem alien to them and people can be afraid of what is unfamiliar.

    I used to work with several individuals who came to a conclusion years ago that they were going to continue using paper files as opposed to electronic documents. The basic argument was that they wanted something tangible; something they could hold on to. They didn't want to learn about electronic files. It was something new and unfamiliar. A certain amount of learning would be required in order for them to catch up with growing technology. The problem they encountered was that many people and companies started using electronic files. It forced them to be put in a very uncomfortable position where they either had to learn something new and more efficient or get bad yearly reviews from their employer. These individuals would spend a decent amount of time talking about the good ole days before all of the internet nonsense. This could have been an opportunity to increase their knowledge and develop the courage to experience something they had never done before but instead they chose to allow doubt to cloud their minds. Unfortunately, the efficiency of their work with paper files was no match for the high speed internet. After a few rounds of complaints from other companies that were relying on the information these paper files contained and a very bad performance review by their employer these individuals resigned. They gave up a career and profession they loved and had profound understanding of just because they were fearful of learning something new.

    What's the point? Use courage to fight against the naysayers and self-doubt. Use courage to battle those thoughts of discouragement. Use courage to put forward the strategies that are laid out in this book and maybe strategies given by other investors who can take you to the next level of financial progress. Don't be the workers who don't even try because of fear and ultimately lose out.

What's the point? Use courage to fight against the naysayers and self-doubt. Use courage to battle those thoughts of discouragement. Use courage to put forward the strategies that are laid out in this book and maybe strategies given by other investors who can take you to the next level of financial progress. Don't be the workers who don't even try because of fear and ultimately lose out.

CHAPTER FOUR

TIME FOR SOME INCREASE

"Goals Reality Options Will"
—UNKNOWN AUTHOR

I don't know what your financial situation is but if you're reading this book I will assume that you are looking to increase where you are financially. Maybe you're looking for some tips for a friend or co-worker. Here's something to consider. The majority of the working poor and middle class are overloaded with bills and debt. For some, it's student loans, car payments, mortgage payments, etc. Some of us are flat lining financially because of credit cards and personal loans. For others, it's just the day-to-day financial burdens that have us suffering, such as rent, groceries, Wi-Fi, healthcare costs, taking the bus, and whatever else you can think of. You can't consider taking your money and investing because there seems to be a whole lot of week left over at the end of your money. In other words, many of us are not even able to make it pay check to pay check.

    This book would do you a big disservice to not mention looking at what you spend your money on and try to figure out where possible cuts can be made. For now, let's just take your expenses as is, without reducing anything. We will use $200/week as a hypothetical number. If you are making $200/week and have expenses of $200/week you have no excess money to invest and therefore have no way of having financial progress. This is where you say "Thanks, Captain Obvious!" You'll need to bring in extra income. For the progress that makes this strategy work you'll need an extra $5/day. So, you'll need to bring home $235/week. Your expenses are still at $200/week. $235-$200= $35 left over.

This $35 is what will be used to catapult your finances to the next level. The following chapters will give you some ideas on how to get that extra $5/day. For most of the suggestions in this book you'll be able to bring home more than an extra $5/day. I know $5 seems like a small amount to some and not enough to take your finances beyond what they've always been.

If you've ever exercised or done physical therapy, part of what you're doing is starting off small and lifting light weights or doing one lap around the track. That one lap leads into two laps and eventually two miles. That two-pound dumbbell turns into a twenty-pound dumbbell after consistent exercise. That $35/week will turn into $500/week. This can happen with consistency. It's like taking a seed and planting it in soil. You must water it consistently. Eventually it'll grow, in its season.

CHAPTER FIVE

AIRBNB

"I WAS A STRANGER AND YOU INVITED ME IN."
—JESUS

Let's talk about the first way where you can generate that extra money every week or month. Airbnb is a great way to do this. The basic premise with Airbnb is that your home becomes its very own hotel room or suite. People who are traveling for business, vacation, or for other reasons can stay at your place, almost as if it were a hotel, minus the room service. Some people who host Airbnb travelers have entire houses to rent out, while some have apartments, and/or rooms to rent as well.

Of course, make sure you do your own due diligence and question asking for individuals who are looking to rent your space through Airbnb. Also, if the space that you are renting to someone from Airbnb is a space that you are leasing yourself you should get permission from the owner/landlord before doing this. It may be required that you modify your current lease agreement slightly to include this provision. I will say that as of right now the individuals that I know who host Airbnb guests and don't own their home but rather live in a leased residence, haven't had any issues with regards to that. As a matter of fact, one person I know has a house that he rents out for Airbnb guests. In his business, instead of *buying* additional real estate and turning them into Airbnb rentals he searches for popular and busy market places that are trendy to tourists and *leases* apartments or houses from owners and then in turn hosts Airbnb guests at those places. This saves him on the major outpouring of money he may have to do with purchasing real estate while at the same time leaving him free and clear from the responsibilities of ownership. Of course, I know someone else who does the exact opposite. He's from Australia and he purchases houses all over and just uses Airbnb.

The Airbnb industry allows hosts to gain financially by charging cleaning fees, security deposits, and other extra fees. Hosts have the option to provide amenities, establish house rules and choose who you will or will not allow in your facility. Before we discuss the profit potential I do want to give a slight disclaimer.

Just a couple words of caution:

1. Be sure to check out the rental laws for your area and make sure it is legal to host an Airbnb guest.

2. If there is a situation where you may have to put out money to get your place ready for Airbnb hosting, such as painting a room or doing some other minor/major work make sure that you're in an area where people would actually want to book. I live in the Northeast Corridor of the country, right in the tri-state area, and booking for me has never been an issue. Many of the hosts that I have come across either live in popular tourist areas or right near airports.

3. Be sure to keep the place orderly, neat, and clean. It is very possible for people to come and stay at your place and write bad reviews if your place looks like a garbage dump or if they encounter a host who is not too cordial. Besides the extra money, which is great, it is truly an opportunity to be successful. As I think of the big picture, I have a continuous

smile. I think of the goal and push forward. I think of the big picture. Think of the goal. Just as you wake up in the morning and already experience success because you've gotten up and have the courage to start the day, you can have success with Airbnb. Keeping this in mind should help drive away any strong thoughts of underperforming.

Now let's talk money. The profit potential for being an Airbnb host is big. The real gain has to do with the fact that you can take a spare room or an unoccupied space and make money off it. Normally it would just be sitting there for maybe old clothes or spare tires or whatever else might go into that space. As an Airbnb host, you've now turned that space that wasn't making you any money into extra cash flow for you. You may think it is too difficult and time consuming to take on this opportunity, but if you are able to be an Airbnb host there is a lot of information about Airbnb available online to help you set up your potential income stream. For example, there is a feature called "Smart Pricing" or "Dynamic Pricing" which gives you an idea about the pricing for your area. If you'd like, it'll set the value for you. You also have the option of setting a minimum and a maximum amount for that feature. In other words, you can put the smart pricing on and if you don't want it to go below a minimum dollar amount you have the option of adjusting to that dollar amount. The same thing works in reverse for the maximum dollar amount when using the smart pricing feature. For example, the smart pricing for your Airbnb space may say $60 per night. For various reasons, you may have determined that you don't want anything less than $65 per night. If A potential Airbnb guest is looking to rent your space for a period of time and the smart pricing is on the guest will see that instead of the pricing being at $60/night it'll be set to $65/night. If you do set the minimum to $65/night and the smart/dynamic pricing suggests $70/night it'll go with the option that will give you more money or profit. In this case, it would be $70/night. There is a lot of information about Airbnb, available online. If you are able to be an Airbnb host I strongly recommend this as an extra form of cash. Of course, you will have to pay taxes on this income and there will be a little bit of extra work that needs to get done but in general this is a great vehicle and starting point to get you to your destination of financial growth.

There was a millennial I was talking to, let's call him Larry, who had over $30,000 in student loan debt and just moved out of his parents' house. He had gotten his first job out of college and was really trying to move ahead financially but felt very much stuck. Larry had a one bedroom apartment in a fairly decent neighborhood. Anyway, we were talking one day and I asked him how much more expensive would it be to get a two or three-bedroom apartment in a nicer area of the same town? He told me that there would be a difference of about $400/month to $500/month to do this. At the time, in that better area of his town, Airbnb pricing for room rentals were at about $50 per night. If he was able to get a three-bedroom apartment and rent out two of the bedrooms to Airbnb guests at $50/room/night x 2 rooms, then he would not only make up the difference in rent but also end up with a good additional monthly revenue stream. That's precisely what he decided to do. The last time Larry volunteered information to me his Airbnb apartment stays at about a 95% occupancy rate. Let's do the math:

1. 30 days in a month x 95% occupancy = 28 to 29 days out of the month his extra rooms are making him $100/night.

2. Larry is bringing in $2800-$2900/month

3. His rental increase from his 1 bedroom to his 3 bedroom was $500/month.

4. He was able to increase his finances by $2300 to $2400/month. This was several months ago, from the time I'm writing this but he has been able to almost finish paying off his student loan debt.

As stated earlier, you can charge cleaning fees for your Airbnb rentals. Since he was just renting out a room then his fee was $20 per visitor. On average Larry was getting about 14 visitors per month between the two rooms that he was renting. Larry did his own cleaning and washing of the linens between guests. It wouldn't take him that long and it wasn't too costly either. About $5 of that cleaning fee was being used for supplies and the other $15 was based on the time that it took for Larry to do the manual task of cleaning and getting set up for the next guest. Let's do some additional math:

1. Besides the $2300 net cash flow Larry had at the end of the month, he also had these cleaning fees that were a positive source of revenue for him.

2. $15/visitor x 14 visitors/month = $210/month

3. In all Larry went from just getting by to profiting over $2500/month ($2300 + $210).

Larry asked for some guidance on what I felt his next steps should be since he was on a great start in paying off his student loan. Larry was already on a path for allowing his money to work for him. He could keep this up and duplicate this method with other apartments or other houses and make an entire business out of this. I did advise Larry to speak to my mutual fund advisor, who is (at the time of me writing this book) with AXA Equitable. I'll get more into mutual funds later in the book but once Larry's looming student loans are paid off his next step will be to allow his money to continue to work for him in the form of mutual funds.

CHAPTER SIX

RIDE SHARING

"WE GOIN' RIDIN' ON THE FREEWAY OF LOVE, IN MY
PINK CADILLAC."
—ARETHA FRANKLIN

It's safe to say that everyone may not find that Airbnb works for their situation. There are other resources available to help increase one's finances. One such way is through some of the rideshare companies such as Uber or Lyft. Most people are very familiar with these two companies. There may be other companies that offer the same type of money making opportunity. Please feel free to research these companies and apply the same concepts that will be laid out in this chapter.

With rideshare companies, you can use your own vehicle to make money. Your own vehicle is basically a taxi minus the yellow cab look that so many of us are familiar with. You will need to make sure the vehicle is in good condition and that you have access to a smart phone. I've interviewed several Uber and Lyft drivers and this stream of income seems to be very profitable. Full disclosure, all the drivers that I have spoken to live or work either near an airport or in a Metropolitan area. In other words, if you don't have access to these areas then this may not be as lucrative a venture for you.

The drivers I've spoken to have said that they make anywhere between $200-$300 per shift. For the most part, these drivers I've spoken to consider shift ranges from 8 to 12 hours of work within a week. That's a pretty good chunk of change. One of the great things about these rideshare companies is that you can make your own schedule. If you only have a couple of extra hours every day to make some extra money, then you can very well be a driver. I know several people who have a full-time job with benefits but work Uber or Lyft on the side for about 20 hours per week. Let's use some realistic numbers:

1. Working two - 10 hour shifts/week could yield $400, according to my discussions with other Uber and Lyft drivers. Remember we are keeping all your current expenses and habits the same.

2. This extra $400/week multiplies out over a year to almost $21,000.00.

Just like Larry, the millennial, in Chapter 5 of Airbnb had to upgrade his living space to bring in $2500 more/month, I know someone who did a similar thing with Uber and Lyft.

Let's call her Gail, the Gen X Uber/Lyft Driver. She wanted to increase her income but worked over 50 hours/week at her full-time job. She wanted to employ some of the methods I'll address later in the book about having her money work for her but was bogged down with bills and other expenses without having much of anything saved at the end of the month. I suggested she drive for Uber or Lyft since they were flexible with schedules. She looked at me as if I had two heads. Why? Because she didn't have a car! Yes, I did know that and was being slightly tongue in cheek when I suggested this.

After I saw the look on Gail's face I chuckled. She asked how she was supposed to drive for Lyft or Uber without something to *drive* in. That was a good question, even though it was one of those rhetorical questions, where you either don't expect a response or you expect a response that is on the ridiculous side. Well I gave her a response. I first asked her about her credit. She said it was "so-so." I then told her that she can get a new car with no money down and have any money that would normally be due rolled into the car payments. "Won't my car payments be higher?" She was absolutely right. Here's the thing: having a car can be a liability and cost you money but if you're using that car to drive for Uber or Lyft and making more money than the expenses of the car then it's no longer a liability but now an asset. In other words, it's allowing you to make money.

Gail and I ran the numbers on how much she could be making from Uber and Lyft and how much the car payments would be approximately. I prefer to stay on the low side with my numbers, in general. In other words if someone says I could make between $200 to $400/day on a deal, when I perform my calculation to see what my profit will most likely be I would use the $200/day amount. Here's the numbers we used for Gail:

1. Car payment and Insurance: $430/month + $180/month = $610/month

2. Gail planned on working 24 hours/week with Lyft and Uber. In her market that averaged about $400-$500/week, sometimes more. Let's be conservative and go with $400/week.

3. $400/week x 52 weeks/year = about $21,000 extra per year.

4. Car payment and insurance per year = $610 x 12 = $7320

5. Her extra income = $21000 - $7320 = $13,680 for the year or $1140 for the month.

Gail had both the intelligence to see that her situation needed to change and the courage to step out and enact that change. Also, because Gail had a goal she didn't complain about working extra. Shortly after Gail started seeing profit from her Uber job she decided to use one of her spare bedrooms for Airbnb. Her monthly cash flow increased an additional $1100/month.

You will notice this suggestion brings you much more than the extra $5/day needed to progress financially. If this financial path seems like it might be right for you, then check their websites for more details. Please note that all the drivers I have spoken to live or work either near an airport or in a Metropolitan area. If you don't have access to these type of areas then this may not be as lucrative for you.

Both Larry and Gail have remarked to me in passing that they feel good waking up every day because each new day represents an opportunity to take another successful step towards their goal. They used their extra money to make bigger investments that didn't require them to do more work. Their money began working for them. It would have been very common place for the two of them to not make any change and complain about their situations. They could have used time and energy wallowing in self-pity and self-doubt, feeling like the universe was somehow unfair to them. They could have focused on all the things they couldn't do as opposed to all the things that could be done. Larry and Gail chose the higher road.

CHAPTER SEVEN

DELIVERY DRIVER

"HOW BEAUTIFUL ON THE MOUNTAIN ARE THE FEET OF THOSE WHO BRING GOOD NEWS."
—ISAIAH

There are all kinds of delivery drivers: pizza, fast food, auto parts, bakery, florist, hardware, grocery, pharmaceutical and the list goes on and on. Depending on where you live and the type of delivery service needed you could easily take on a delivery job.

Often these types of jobs are missed opportunities to increase your weekly take home pay. However, delivery jobs have the potential for greatness. There are companies that will supply you with transportation to make their deliveries. But many times, or at least based on my experiences, the delivery person is responsible for providing the transportation. As far as pay is concerned, a good portion of companies pay minimum-wage. The thing is that these jobs normally come with tips, so whoever you are delivering to may give you extra money for delivering their item. Another benefit to these jobs is the flexibility of scheduling. I've spoken to a number of delivery drivers who were able to pick their own schedules. For me, in order to pay for graduate school I worked at a store called Planet Wings and my start off pay was $7/hour. My shift ranged from 4 to 6 hours. I averaged about 8 deliveries per hour and each delivery tipped me approximately $3. Sometimes it would be more and sometimes a little bit less. In an hour, I made about $24 in tips and an extra $7 for my base pay. I tended to not take many breaks during my shift to make better use of my time. Whenever a delivery was ready to go out I was on top of it. Sometimes I even helped the people at the register pack the bags. If you decide that this is the route you would like to take please know that the numbers I described in this example are based on *my* own experiences. If a delivery job pays less it's OK. Remember, this is a means to earning at least $5 more /day than you already do, so that you can invest that money. One thing I'd like to note is that I scheduled myself for the busy times during the week, such as Friday evening, Saturday afternoon/evening and Sunday afternoon. My take home pay was over $360/week, with this job. Let's do the math:

1. $360/week x 52 weeks/year = $18720

2. This breaks down to $1560/month I invested into my mutual fund accounts at a growth of about 10%/year.

3. I paid for graduate school three times in a year: 12 months/3 times = Every four months I would pay for graduate school

4. $1560/month x 4 months @ 10%/year interest = $7984.

5. The interest I made was $184. This purchased my books for the next semester and the amount saved covered me taking two classes/semester. Unlike undergraduate, I graduated with two degrees and no debt.

Being a delivery driver is another way of generating extra income so that money can then be invested and then used to generate more money without you working more. There are only 24 hours in a day and I'm sure you wouldn't want to work that much any way. Besides the fact that you need a social life it just wouldn't be healthy for your mind or body. The delivery job was never meant to be an ongoing thing for me, although it could've been. The money didn't go into a bank and just sit there until my term bill came. The money went into an aggressive 529 plan, which consists of mutual funds that allows for tax breaks on the interest you make. The money made from a 529 plan must be used for educational purposes to qualify for the tax breaks. In my case it was used for graduate school.

I worked hard during that period to generate the money I needed to invest into graduate school. I'll get into education as an investment in a later chapter but just a quick note: your education is very much a worthwhile investment. Your learning/education is not limited to getting a high school, college, or post graduate degree. It can consist of reading books or attending seminars. My plumber who has a GED, makes $200/hour and that's the very discounted rate he gives to me because we have a good business relationship. He went to trade school and became a master plumber through his pursuit of education. His investment in learning a trade helped to increase his financial situation. Do you know how he paid for trade school: Delivering pizzas!

CHAPTER EIGHT

LANDSCAPING AND PROPERTY MAINTENANCE

Landscaping and Property Maintenance represents a very broad range of tasks. It can involve gardening, grass cutting, bush and tree trimming, handy person services, snow removal, leaf removal, garbage removal, painting etc. I know a person who enjoys being outdoors in the Spring, Summer, and Fall. He decided to take a few hours on Saturday and Sunday to cut people's lawns and hedges. Within an hour he is able to take care of four properties. The properties are right next to one another. He charges around $50/property which is approximately $200/hour. He has about 4 hours' worth of work every weekend. Let's do the math:

1. He services 4 houses/hour.

2. He charges $50/house.

3. 4 x $50 = $200/hour.

4. At minimum, he works 4 hours on the weekend.

5. $200/hour x 4 hours = $800/week at minimum.

Going back to economy of scale, the person who has a lawn mowing business on the side started with a gas-powered lawn mower and some manual hedge trimmers. He was able to get this side business going for under $300. Likewise, I have a snow removal company. One year, I was laid off from my job of 13 years. Thankfully I had my snow removal company and there was plenty of snow that year. I started my snow removal business with a $15 shovel and a $5 bag of salt. I have other people working for the business but I have so much business that I turn down work because I don't have enough people to service all the properties. Every time it snows in the Northeast I make approximately $1000 of clear profit, at a minimum.

By the way, that money goes directly into a place of growth and financial progress. Just to give you a hint, it snowed 5 times during the last winter season. My profit was well over $5000. I took $1000 of that and split it between a charity and some people I knew who were struggling at the time. The remaining $4000 went into a mutual fund that began yielding me roughly 20% yearly return, which was a little over an additional $800 that year. The $20 I initially put into snow removal has given me thousands of dollars of interest payments. This is money that I haven't had to work for but more so has worked for me and continues to do so.

One other important note is about giving and helping. If you allow it, this book can change your financial life. This book coupled with your courage and intelligence can not only be a great help to you, the reader, but should and could also be a help to someone else, who may not have access to this book. Please pay it forward. A noteworthy quote from the bible is *"Give and you will receive. Your gift will return to you in full-pressed down shaken together to make room for more, running over and poured into your lap."* In other words, share this knowledge and share in the financial rewards you'll reap from this. Whether you're painting porches or chopping wood you can turn your situation around but as best as possible make sure you reach back to help others. The person who gives also receives. Writer,

Amanda MacMillan, wrote an article for *TIME Health* which outlined scientific research that showed being generous improves overall health and life expectancy.

CHAPTER NINE

TAKING PICTURES FOR BPO COMPANIES AND REAL ESTATE REFERRALS

"USE A PICTURE. IT'S WORTH A THOUSAND WORDS."
—TESS FLANDERS

Out of all the ways, that I've named so far to boost your income, these two are most likely the easiest. Let me explain first what a BPO company is. A BPO (Broker Price Opinion) is a price evaluation on real estate, for example a house or a building. Many times, a BPO is associated with foreclosure homes and pre-foreclosure homes but can be any piece of real estate. It's not as involved as an appraisal but similar. Companies and banks normally hire a broker to give an opinion on how much the property in question is worth. The broker normally understands the market area, where the property is located. Part of this evaluation consists of taking pictures.

This is where you and your smart phone come in. There are real estate companies that need people to take pictures of property and email/upload those pictures back to the real estate company. Just Google BPO Photography jobs and you'll most likely get a whole lot of results. You can also go on Craigslist.com to find those kinds of jobs. If you know any real estate companies in your area just walk in and ask. A lot of times their agents and brokers are busy selling homes and don't have time to run around snapping pictures of houses. This job is normally very flexible and pays between $6/house to $40/house. For the most part you need a cellphone with a camera and internet and you're all set. An associate of mine, let's call him Rodney, takes these pictures. On average Rodney takes 7-8 pictures of houses/day. The company Rodney works for pays him between $8 and $15 per house. All of these are in a 10-15-mile radius of where Rodney works or lives. Yes, Rodney has a full-time job but wanted to make a little extra money to help go towards some property he wanted to buy. I asked him about how long does it take on average to do this job. He told me that in order to take pictures of seven different properties it takes a little over an hour. Let's do the math for Rodney. I'm going to use the lowest numbers to calculate this:

1. $8/house x 7 houses/day x 6 days/week

2. 8x7x6=$336/week extra

3. $336/week x 52 weeks/year = $17,472.00 extra for the year

Ironically, Rodney purchased an investment property after a year. The irony is that one of the very properties he took pictures of he bought. Rodney's story doesn't end there. He took the extra $336/week and added it to a mutual fund where the money grew until he found a good investment property. He bought a 4-family house for $74,000 that needed a little work. In the area where the investment property was located Rodney was able to rent out each apartment for $1,000/month. Rodney's mortgage, including the taxes and insurance he pays on the house, come to just under $1,000/month.

Rodney still works the BPO picture job because he gets paid to look at future investments, as he puts it, but also has a yearly financial gain from his 4-family investment property of $36,000.00.

Let's go over what just happened, real quick:

1. Rodney used his cell phone and his car to make over $17,472.00 extra per year

2. He took the extra money and invested in a mutual fund that paid about 8%/year.

3. He took the extra money after one year, which grew to $18,248, and bought a 4-family investment house

4. The 4-family brings in $3,000 extra every month

5. $36,000 + $18,248 = $54,248

Regarding real estate referrals, many times agents and brokers will give you a referral for telling them about a customer who needs to buy or sell property. On average, I've seen people get anywhere from $50-$300/referral. It depends on where you live of course but if you live in an apartment complex sometimes the landlord/management will offer one month free rent or half off for referrals. For the tenants I currently have as well as ones I've had in the past I have always offered a referral of a few hundred dollars if I needed a new renter. Landlords do not want any of their properties sitting vacant. So many times, they will go above and beyond to get vacancies filled. Do your best to make sure that the referral is a decent person. You don't want to refer someone and they are a nightmare to deal with.

A similar referral bonus happens for people looking for loans. People can be paid a fee for referring a good customer to them. I do know some people who just do referrals for a living. Some people do it for a part time gig. Currently, I have a referral arrangement with a mortgage company and for every person I refer who completes a loan with this company, I receive $250. Some companies pay $500/referral. Some pay more. I won't get into it in this book but there are real estate lenders called "Hard Money Lenders." They are called this because they give loans on houses that need more than the average repairs. Most hard money lenders I've come across have this referral program where they'll pay $100 to $500/referral.

Let's look at an acquaintance of mine who we will call Suzie. Suzie has a job in marketing. She meets a lot of people throughout her workday and has an overall great attitude. In her day-to-day activities she comes across people who need homes to buy or places to rent. Suzie was interested in growing her money and wanted enough money to invest in a business. She made approximately $400/referral through a real estate company she had a good business relationship with. Suzie set a goal of 10 referrals/month. As of the time I'm writing this, she averages 12 referrals/month. I would say that Suzie is successful. She made a goal and surpassed it. She mapped out the strategy then carried out her plan. While she waited to get the amount of money together to invest in this particular business she put the referral money into a mutual fund which gave her about 13% interest per year. Let's do the math:

1. $400/referral

2. 12 referrals/month

3. $400 x 12 referrals = $4800/month

4. $4800/month x 12 months = $57,600.00/year extra

5. 13% interest on $4800, compounded monthly = $61,822.00

6. By year two Suzie had $132,177 in the mutual fund account.

Notice something here: If Suzie continued with the extra money and put it into a regular bank account or underneath her mattress she would have $115,800. Having her money work for her caused an extra $16,000 to be in her account.

CHAPTER TEN

TEACH SOMETHING YOU LOVE

Each and every one of us has that one thing, at least, that we really enjoy doing. I guess we can refer to it as a hobby. Sometimes we are lucky enough to make those hobbies into jobs where we can actually get paid. I know getting paid for something that you love doing is something that rarely happens. But it is a possibility. It may not be your full-time gig but can certainly be a vehicle to help get you to a place of financial progression. Take a little bit of time to figure out what you really love doing. Maybe you've been doing it for a long time but just never thought about getting paid for it.

For everything that one person really enjoys there are many people who would love to learn how to do that particular thing. For some people, they enjoy martial arts and likewise become part time Martial Arts teachers; for some it's dance; for some it's cooking; for some it's carpentry; for others it's roller skating, and so on. Many times, coaches end up coaching something they also enjoy themselves and will get paid for it. They get a sense of satisfaction because they are not only participating in what they love but they are also teaching others and helping to refine the skills of others in that same hobby. I've seen the pay go from $10/hour up to $35/hour depending on what kind of knowledge you're sharing. Either way this will give you more than enough money for your extra $5/day goal. Think about this: you are doing something that you love, getting paid for it, and sharing your knowledge and experiences with someone else.

CHAPTER ELEVEN

YOUR $5 GOAL

I'm sure one of the suggestions from the previous chapters can be used to reach that five dollars extra per day mark. Most of those things that I mentioned had the ability to bring in hundreds of dollars extra per week. My task in this book is to get you from the $0/week investor to the $500 per week investor. The suggestions outlined above are ways that can do just that. Let's discuss what to do with the money now that you've increased your income.

The extra $5 will be used to start a mutual fund account. In the past you had to have several thousand dollars before you were able to start a mutual fund. A mutual fund is an investment tool that is made up of other types of securities such as bonds, stock, and money markets. I'm not an expert in mutual funds by the way. Please make sure you speak to a financial adviser and accountant before investing. You can email me if you need help in picking one out. The great thing with mutual funds is since they are made up of a pool of different investment types, the risk tends to be lower, especially when compared to other investment vehicles. The other great thing is the fact that they offer a much better return than the normal bank account. At the time of me writing this book, having your money in a checking or savings account doesn't give much interest at all. Your money is just sitting there being used by the bank and you are gaining practically nothing for it. Most banks pay you anywhere from .01% to 1% interest per year. That means if you have $100 in your account and it gives you interest of .01% then after one year the bank will pay you

1 cent. At the whopping 1% interest rate the bank will pay you 1 dollar. Normally in order to get that 1% percent interest rate you must have an account with anywhere from $1000 to $5000 in it, sometimes more. Your $5/day would be better spent elsewhere.

A mutual fund company like Acorns or Stash is where you can put that $5/day or $25-$30/week. You have to connect your bank account as well as your debit/credit card to Stash or Acorns. There's a way you can set the account to automatically pull a specific amount of money every week from your bank account. You can set these companies to pull more than $25-$30 if possible. I encourage you to do so, actually. As a matter of fact, as you see the money gained from accounts such as Acorns or Stash, think of ways to put more than the $5/day in there. You can open an Acorns account with 0$. At this point it charges $1/month. Often times they have promotions that give you $5-$10 when you sign up.

Acorns basically takes the money you spend and rounds up the change to the nearest dollar. They use a term called "round-ups" which means when you spend money using a debit card or credit card Acorns takes the difference between the money you spent and the next whole dollar amount and adds that money into a mutual fund account for you, automatically. Let's take a look at an example:

1. Let's pretend you buy a bottle of soda for $1.25.

2. The next whole dollar amount is $2.00.

3. Acorns takes the difference between $2 & $1.25 => $2 - $1.25 = $.75 (75 cents).

4. Acorns will take that 75 cents and put it in a mutual fund account.

You'll never have to worry about that "$5,000" that my father never made. Acorns is almost like a piggy bank or one of those big water jugs that people throw loose change in, except you get an actual return on your money. In other words, your money is working for you. At the time of me writing this, I've averaged about 5% return on the money that has gone into my Acorns account. Again, the appeal has to do with the fact that this would be pocket change that many of us would lose in the first place. Just to recap, the extra $25-$30/week would be automatically transferred and at the same time round-ups would be taking place as well. I don't encourage it but you can turn the rounds-ups or auto deposits off, at any time.

Acorns gives you five different choices as far as types of mutual funds to place your money:

1. Conservative

2. Moderately Conservative

3. Moderate

4. Moderately Aggressive

5. Aggressive

As you go from Conservative to Aggressive the risk increases. This means the mutual fund may progressively have more investments that could increase or decrease rapidly causing a greater chance for losing money. I'm not a financial advisor so I'm not directing you to go with one mutual fund over the other. I'll let you know what I chose.

I decided on fund # 5, Aggressive. With fund # 5 your risk is greater but the chances of you increasing your return, i.e. your profit, is also greater. Also, the amount of your profit is greater potentially also.

Of course, there's still the opportunity for you to see a greater amount of profit (or return on your investment) with a conservative fund but the tendency is for the more aggressive fund do give you the highest profit. Besides the fact that choosing the Aggressive fund would most likely get me the best profits, since I was only investing spare change I didn't really have much to lose.

Stash works differently than Acorns. You can start this account with $5. Stash is an app also but there are no round-ups as in Acorns. I recommend doing a $25 weekly withdrawal that comes out automatically. Also, make sure you do your own research on the requirements of the accounts. Stash does give you more variety as far as types of mutual funds you can invest your money in. Before you invest with either Stash or Acorns try to gain some knowledge about mutual funds if they are new to you. There are mutual fund gurus on YouTube as well as in a Google search. Take a look at some of the info so you can increase your learning.

One of the other great things about both Acorns and Stash is that some of the mutual funds pay dividends on top of the interest the company pays. A dividend is money that a company pays to its shareholders (i.e. people who own parts of the company) from the profits that company makes. Whether you invest in acorns or in stash or in both that $5/day of seed money will grow 24 hours/day and 7 days/week. Here are how the numbers would look best on the returns that I have gotten from these companies:

1. $5/day (5 days/week) auto deposit into Acorns or Stash at 5% return

2. After 1 year of $25/week you'll have about $1344 saved.

3. About $36 of that will be from interest.

4. This is excluding interest from round-ups and dividends.

The temptation might be to say that it's only $1344 and that the interest was only $36. Try to consider two things if this thought pops in your mind: The first thing to consider is that this is $1344 more than you would have had. Also, this money might have been loose change and lost or mistakenly thrown away but instead this money was used to make money. You've come to a place where your money is working for you.

In the beginning, I mentioned making you into the $500/week investor. Don't worry. I haven't forgotten.

CHAPTER TWELVE

THE $500/WEEK INVESTOR

That $1344 that you grew over the past year can be used to put towards any of those earlier ideas such as purchasing equipment for landscaping and property maintenance; putting a down payment on a vehicle to do delivery driving; increasing your apartment size for Airbnb. All the ideas that I mentioned in the first portion of the book have the potential to bring in a few hundred dollars per week. The sole purpose of that money is to invest with it.

Assuming you used one of the ideas mentioned earlier or maybe some other idea that's bringing in $300 per week let's see what the math gives us:

1. $300/week x 52 weeks/year

2. 5% Compounding interest over this year

3. Amount at the end of the year is $16037 with about $430 being made from interest.

4. If you continue the same habits which I urge you to do then by the end of the second year you'll have close to $33,000

Notice that even with you starting at five dollars per day within three years you've moved to being a $500/week investor, at minimum. When you divide $33000 by 52 weeks you get approximately $635/week. At this point it'll be safe to begin investing with a trusted brokerage firm. The one I use is called AXA Equitable.

At this point in time, AXA isn't paying me to promote this. The purpose of this book is to help draw a roadmap based on my own experiences of how I went from a $0/week investor to a $500/week investor. Of course, I asked my financial advisor to put my money into an aggressive fund. Eventually, between my Acorns account and Stash account, I maintained a minimum of $300/week deposit and $1500/month deposits with AXA. One thing to note about AXA is that you can start making mutual fund deposits of $100 twice/month. Once my AXA Equitable account hit over $5000 I started noticing returns of close to 14%/year.

If you need the contact information for the financial advisor that I use at AXA please send me an email. I'll send you his name and contact information.

Let's say you can save an extra $5/day but for whatever reason you can't get to that point of doing landscaping, Uber, referrals, etc. Let's do the math just using $5/day (i.e. $25/week):

1. Year One of $5/day @ 5% interest/year (i.e. $25/week) = $1300

2. Year Two = $2740

3. Year Three = $4215

4. Year Four = $5767

5. Year Five = $7398

6. Year Ten= $16892

7. Year Twenty = $44713

At the Year Ten mark you can switch to a mutual fund that can possibly yield 12-20%. If you have a child or *are* a child and start at the age of 10 then by the time you are 30 you'll potentially have close to $45000. Over $18,800 of that will be from interest! This is a win-win strategy. In other words, even if you do nothing except $5/day you will still have enough by year ten to purchase an investment property or a vehicle for a ride share business or to upgrade your apartment for Airbnb or whatever the next room share business will be.

A lot of times we may feel stuck in our financial situation. Just because you *feel* stuck doesn't mean you *are* stuck. Here's another story for you: Don't worry it's a quick one. I know a lady who is a single mother of two. She works two full time jobs and had no time to Uber or do landscaping or anything else that will take her outside of the home. She wanted to improve her financial situation but her time was stretched to the max as far as working outside of the home. If I tell you she has gifted hands when it comes to food I'm under stating things. Her home cooked meals are delicious. We had a potluck at work. I had the luxury of tasting some of her cooking. This was some years ago. We managed to stay in touch, however. When she expressed some of her financial and family issues I spoke to her about investing and how to get to the next level of $0/day to $500/week. I suggested making dinners to earn that extra money she needed for investing and financial progress. She began making dinners for people. Her thought was that she had to cook any way so why not make a little more for others who may desire a homecooked meal. She began her business with a handful of customers. Her two children helped out with the cooking which allowed them to spend more time together. Her side business became so popular that she left the second full time job. Getting to that point took her less than four months. I do want to emphasize that she has a wonderful attitude about life, especially considering the situation that she was in. It goes back to that popular saying, "Your attitude determines your altitude." She purchased three vehicles and is using them for a rideshare/car rental company named Turo. I've been told by her and some others that Turo is the Airbnb of cars. Just to finish this thought, each car she has through Turo brings in roughly $700/month of net profit. Her goal is to get to ten vehicles. She also has more time with her children and they enjoy the strengthened bond of working together towards a common goal, making homemade dinners. The irony is that I suggested the dinners to her and later she suggested Turo to me. No matter your position in life be open to learning.

Quite often I hear people give reasons why they can't do something even when someone else is pointing out reasons why they *can* do that very thing. The people I've seen who are open to learning tend not to be so closed to certain possibilities. Learning also helps with our overall attitude. If you think of your interactions with people and new ideas as an opportunity for learning and growing then having a bad attitude becomes more difficult. Being negative becomes more difficult when you see that through learning there's the potential for greatness in every minute of the day and every interaction. Use learning to fight against negative thoughts.

CHAPTER THIRTEEN

IF AT FIRST YOU DON'T SUCCEED

At this point in the book you may be excited or at the very least thinking about some of the strategies you can use to progress financially. Those are great thoughts to have. I spoke to a young man, maybe 21 or so, who is in the process of increasing his credit score. He wants to purchase real estate and by having a higher credit score he will have a lower interest rate on the loan that he will need to take out. The more he shared and spoke about his financial journey and plans for the future the more excited he became. It's funny because the reason we crossed paths had to do with me giving him a deposit for an event that I needed him to DJ at. I had some other commitments as did he so we didn't get a chance to finish our wonderful discussion. I wrote him out a check for the deposit and in his excitement, he left the check! I realized this and called him immediately before he drove too far away. As he pulled up after driving around the block we both laughed hysterically because we knew that the excitement coming from him due to our discussion caused us both to forget about his check, which was the sole purpose for us meeting in the first place. He shared with me something that you will experience also, which is a daily excitement that comes with waking up every day with a goal in place. Every day represented another step closer to his goal. It wasn't always like that for him. He came up pretty rough. He had some setbacks in his life. With all the stressors he experienced he was still able to rise above this and get on his road to financial progress. He shared with me that his journey was not only being done for himself but for his mother and the many people he is connected to. This not only gives him excitement for a short period of time but gives him a long-lasting sense of fulfillment, knowing that his life is purpose filled and that his journey will not only be for the benefit of him but for others as well.

I shared the story of the young DJ because I wanted to point out that even with the successes you experience on your journey of financial progress there may be some setbacks. Maybe something doesn't go as planned, financially. There may be some personal setbacks, such as sickness or loss of someone you care about. In other words, life happens. The biggest setbacks I've experienced are in my own mind. Even though I've seen great successes, I have had my share of failures.

My latest failure cost me thousands of dollars. There was a company promising returns of 12% every month. The economy of scale was fine for me. I needed $10000 to start investing with this company. I was excited. If this worked out then I could invest more and possibly get some friends and family involved also. Well, I told certain family and friends about this opportunity and after I received my first monthly check from the company for investing in them, one of my friends invested as well as a close family member. Here's when things got crazy. A few days after that the owner of the business skipped town with the money. The investors in this business were left with fake documentation. We were scammed, basically. How was I going to call both my friend and my family member and explain this disappointment? The first thing I did once I came to grips with what happened was to pray and ask that I don't sink into a depression and that I can have the words to say to my friend and family member.

I made the phone calls and explained the situation. I sincerely apologized and let them know that I contacted the authorities. It wasn't so much the loss of thousands of dollars that really got me down. It was the feeling that I had broken the trust of people I cared about and led them down a path where they each lost $10000. As I drove home, I thought about what store I should stop at to buy a bag full of chocolate and drown myself in sorrow. I was really feeling low. With all the successes I've had with investing and with motivating others I was really ready to give up on the whole notion of financial progress. Imagine that. One bad thing happens and I was ready to throw in the towel. The truth of the matter was that at that moment it wasn't just one bad thing. It was *another* failure. It's interesting how when one bad thing goes wrong at a moment in time we take all of the mess-ups and failures and let downs and heap them onto that one moment and allow that to become the story of our life. Countless people I've spoken to have felt that way at one point in their life. They could have come first place in the races 100 times but that one time they come in last or don't do as well causes them to go into a dark and lonely place. I know these feelings we have at times are natural. The danger is in staying like that. It's dangerous to convince ourselves that these setbacks should define our lives in both the present and the future. My greatest enemy has been "in-a-me." Another way to put it is that my own way of thinking at times has caused missed opportunities and bad decisions. It was my fear of failure. Fear is also natural. It keeps us safe and prevents a lot of things from hurting us. That is considered healthy fear. For instance, if we want to go swimming but know there are sharks in the water then fear will tell us that probably isn't a good idea. So having a certain level of fear is healthy.

Fear shouldn't be your go-to emotion, however. Just because you've experienced setbacks in areas of your life you shouldn't just give up and say that this setback will be something that limits you forever. I was in fact getting ready to throw in the towel but I began thinking about the various people I've helped and how their lives have been enriched. I thought about my own struggles and things I've had to overcome. The common themes that the people I've met and wrote about in this book all shared a good attitude and a willingness to never ever give up. I also remembered how with every setback I was able to learn and grow. That's why I want to emphasize again to continue learning. Remember our guy from Chapter 2 who wanted to go to the beach with his buds. There were several different things he had to figure out in order to make it to the beach. It's the same thing with life. Set a goal. You may run into some setbacks on your journey but setbacks are normally temporary and have ways to get around them and try something different. The silver lining to that story of me getting scammed was that I found an investment where I'm making an extra $1800/month and will have the opportunity to make more. Instead of using the time and energy on feeling sorry for myself I put the energy into a different strategy that has taken me a step further down my road of financial progress. There is a lot of company you can keep on this financial journey. Don't have fear be one of your companions.

CHAPTER FOURTEEN

THE VALUE OF EDUCATION

I mentioned in a previous chapter that one of the things I invested in was my education. I educated myself on real estate, mutual funds, stock, and stock options. At the beginning of my journey I had a bachelor's degree. That's a great degree to have however in my field of work I was limited due to my degree. Therefore, once I had enough money through mutual funds and my investment strategies I went into graduate school. When you invest in your education not only are you opening your mind to additional learning but you are also potentially putting yourself in a situation where you can earn more money. With that definition alone your education can be viewed as a financial investment. Once I finished with both of my graduate degrees my income more than doubled within the year. I spent close to $60,000 for that education but have earned way more than that since getting my graduate degrees. In my case, it was graduate school but as I said before it can be increasing your education when it comes to a trade or some sort of craft or maybe even a hobby.

There are very little limits on what you can do potentially. When we are young we have wild and creative imaginations which can take us to unnamed planets and galaxies. It allows us to see unicorns in the clouds and dream big dreams. The limits on our minds are the ones that *we* allow to be placed. The ideas contained in this book can be carried out by preteens. I'm not talking about buying real estate or driving for Uber but more so the idea of the possibilities of greatness and progressing financially. I was nine years old when I started my first job along with my good friend Damien. During the summertime, we went from door to door with our lawnmower and hedge trimmers asking people if they wanted us to take care of their lawn for them. We did quite well that summer. There was a whole lot of video game money earned. We were just sitting around talking one day and decided to go for it. It was intelligence and courage combined to do something that was fairly new to us. That's all you need: intelligence and courage. Get the idea and the courage to carry out the idea. Sure, there may be times when you try an idea and it doesn't work out. Going back to our definition of success, even though an idea may not have completely worked out this time there was success just in the fact that the idea was put into action. Also, let yourself know that there will be future success as you get ready to try the next idea.

Two other things that I'd like to mention before ending: creating a budget will help you keep track of where your money is going. It will assist you in setting future financial goals. One of the worst things that you can do is to do nothing, but a close second is to do something without any structure organization. You can end up sabotaging all of your efforts. I will gladly send a budget template as an Excel file for anyone interested. My email address will be located in the back of the book. In the Subject of the email put in the following wording **"Request for Budget Template."** There will be a small cost associated with getting the template. There are also apps for smart phones that can help you create and keep a budget. I've seen several ones that are free. Pocket Expense is a good app to use for budgeting.

Lastly, your character is very important. Your work ethic is tied to your character. All the suggestions that have been laid out in this book regarding making extra income have been successful partly due to the work ethic of the individuals looking to progress financially. To the best of your ability, stay focused on the bigger picture because it will help your attitude. Once you start seeing the fruit of your extra effort you will find a sense of motivation growing within. The names mentioned in this book are people who were ordinary in their circumstance but extraordinary in their attitude. They were open to new ideas. That openness propelled them from being in debt and depressed by their circumstances to being excited to wake up every day because each day was a reminder of how far they had come in their five-dollar journey.

Anomaly1977@outlook.com

www.ingramcontent.com/pod-product-compliance
Lightning Source LLC
Chambersburg PA
CBHW031543210526
45464CB00003B/1120